PURE & SIMPLE

Pure & Simple

17 Primitive Projects Inspired by the Seasons

Maggie Bonanomi

Martingale
Create with Confidence

Pure & Simple: 17 Primitive Projects Inspired by the Seasons
© 2018 by Maggie Bonanomi

Martingale®
19021 120th Ave. NE, Ste. 102
Bothell, WA 98011-9511 USA
ShopMartingale.com

Printed in China
23 22 21 20 19 18   8 7 6 5 4 3 2 1

**Library of Congress Cataloging-in-Publication Data is
available upon request.**

ISBN: 978-1-60468-901-3

MISSION STATEMENT

We empower makers who use fabric and yarn
to make life more enjoyable.

CREDITS

**PUBLISHER AND
CHIEF VISIONARY OFFICER**
Jennifer Erbe Keltner

CONTENT DIRECTOR
Karen Costello Soltys

DESIGN MANAGER
Adrienne Smitke

MANAGING EDITOR
Tina Cook

PRODUCTION MANAGER
Regina Girard

ACQUISITIONS EDITOR
Karen M. Burns

STUDIO PHOTOGRAPHER
Brent Kane

TECHNICAL EDITOR
Karen Bolesta

LOCATION PHOTOGRAPHER
Adam Albright

COPY EDITOR
Sheila Chapman Ryan

ILLUSTRATOR
Maggie Bonanomi

Contents

Introduction

Color and design are very important to me, as is simplicity. I don't take myself or my designs too seriously. They are meant to be fun and in no way perfect; in fact, what I love about many of the old wool mats and hooked rugs is the spontaneous manner in which they were made. I can imagine that the women who lovingly crafted these remarkable items used what they had on hand and made something—even with limited design skills—for the pure joy of it and often the pure necessity.

Wool comes in many forms; I've used wool from clothing found in closets and purchased from thrift stores, and I even eyed a lovely wool blazer someone was wearing! Look for labels that say 100% wool and always wash any wool before you use it. That said, I like to use hand-dyed wool because of the color variations you might get in each piece. One thing you'll find interesting is the variation within the same color when the wool is dyed on different days. This adds to the charm, if you ask me. I like the consistent colors I find in wool from Blackberry Primitives, so I use their color names for the projects in the book. I also have included a list of generic color names (see page 94), and you're welcome to change the wool colors to your liking.

When I began doing appliqué nearly 25 years ago, I did not live near a quilt shop so I used what I could find locally. I have always used Coats and Clark thread in the color Summer Brown (except when I stitched a white-on-white bedcover and used Ecru). It's a great neutral thread, and I figure that mid-nineteenth-century women may have had the choice of only light and dark thread—unless they were wealthy and could afford bright colors. I've seen early quilts that are stitched with what I'd call string!

From Little Brown Bird (page 9) to Life Is Good (page 89), these projects will take you through the different seasons and all through the year. I hope you love these designs and, most of all, I hope you have fun!

Maggie

Little Brown Bird

I am sure this plump little bird has eaten a few too many seeds and berries, but she will happily hang here in the tree branches and hold your pins while you sit and stitch.

FINISHED PIN KEEP: 5¼" × 7½"

Materials

I used wool from Blackberry Primitives (see "Resources" on page 95). To help you re-create this project, the materials list gives the exact color names for the wool I used.

- 6" × 8½" piece of Pear wool for front and leaves
- 6" × 8½" piece of tan plaid homespun cotton for back
- 4" × 7" piece of Hazelnut wool for bird body
- 2½" × 4" piece of Old Ivory wool for wing
- 1" × 2" piece of Black wool for spots and eye
- 1" × 1" square of Boulder wool for legs
- 1" × 1" square of Old Straw wool for beak
- Cotton stuffing
- 1 yard of cord for hanger
- 1 twig, 9" long
- Hand-sewing supplies (see page 93)
- Freezer paper for transferring patterns

Cutting

Referring to "Wool Techniques" on page 93, use freezer paper and the patterns on page 11 to trace and then cut the front, back, and appliqués.

From the Pear wool, cut:
1 front
2 leaves

From the homespun, cut:
1 back

From the Hazelnut wool, cut:
1 bird

From the Old Ivory wool, cut:
1 wing

From the Black wool, cut:
3 spots
1 eye

From the Boulder wool, cut:
2 legs

From the Old Straw wool, cut:
1 beak

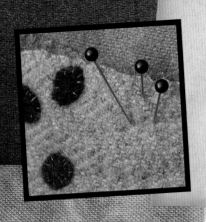

I meant to do my work today—
But a brown bird sang in the apple tree,
And a butterfly flitted across the field,
And all the leaves were calling me.

~ Richard Le Gallienne

Appliquéing the Pin Keep

1. Position the bird on the wool front and pin in place; refer to the photo on page 8 for placement guidance.

2. Using Summer Brown or coordinating thread and a hand-sewing needle, whipstitch in place; leave small openings to insert the beak and legs. Position the wing; pin and whipstitch in place.

3. Tuck the beak and legs slightly underneath the bird appliqué and whipstitch in place. Position the spots and eye and whipstitch in place.

4. To add accent stitching, use a running stitch to create definition in the wing and tail; see page 11.

Birdology

My Little Brown Bird pin keep is a simple project, but if you like, you can embellish the bird with stitches using embroidery floss or pearl cotton—and even wool thread. Change her to a bluebird or a red-winged blackbird. Or add eggs and a nest of wool strips in browns along the curved edge to make a perfect perch for a nest.

Assembling the Pin Keep

1. With right sides together, stitch the front and back together using a ¼" seam allowance and leaving a 3" opening along the straight edge for turning. Turn right side out, stuff, and whipstitch the opening closed.

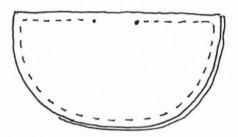

Leave 3" opening.

2. Attach the pin keep to the twig by sewing through the upper corners of the pin keep and wrapping thread around the twig multiple times; securely knot the thread.

3. Stack the leaves and whipstitch around the edges. Use a running stitch to create a leaf vein.

4. Cut the cord in half. Tie the doubled cord to each end of the twig to make a hanger. Stitch the leaf to the cord as an accent.

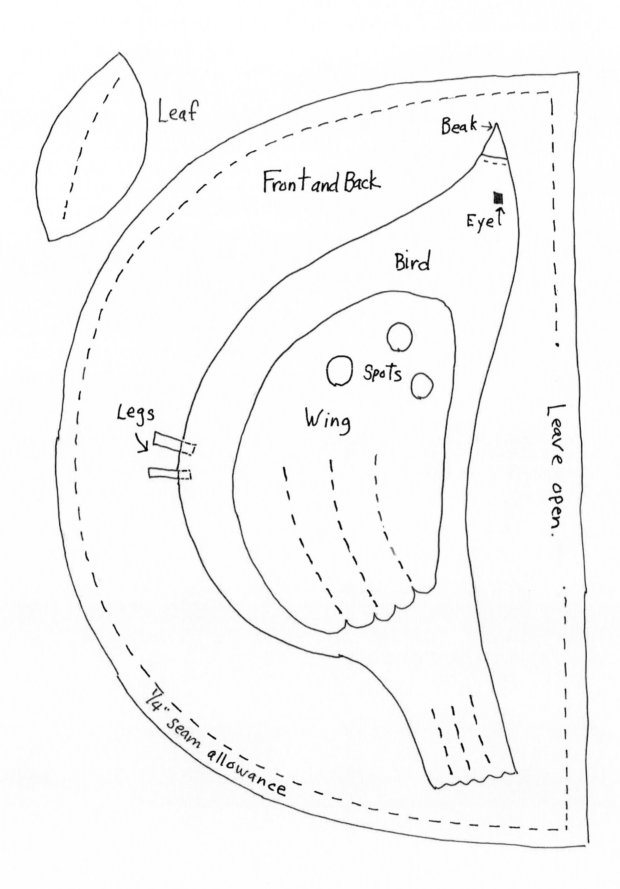

Leaf

Front and Back

Beak →

Eye ↑

Bird

Spots

Wing

Legs

1/4" seam allowance

Leave open.

White Tulips

I am particularly fond of white tulips, especially in the wintertime; they seem as calm and quiet as a snowfall. Tulips are very graceful, and they continue to grow even after they're cut, giving them a lovely swanlike arch to their stems.

FINISHED PILLOW: 7½" × 10½"

Materials

I used wool from Blackberry Primitives (see "Resources" on page 95). To help you re-create this project, the materials list gives the exact color names for the wool I used.

- 8" × 11" piece of Tobacco wool for pillow front
- 8" × 11" piece of dark-colored cotton for pillow back
- 1¾" × 8" strip of Pear wool for stems
- 2½" × 10" piece of Parchment wool for tulips
- Cotton stuffing
- 14" length of ½"-wide aqua ribbon
- Hand-sewing supplies (see page 93)
- Freezer paper for transferring patterns

Cutting

Referring to "Wool Techniques" on page 93, use freezer paper and the pattern on page 15 to trace and then cut the tulip appliqués.

From the Pear wool, cut:
6 strips, ¼" × 8"; crosscut into:
    1 strip, ¼" × 5½"
    1 strip, ¼" × 6"
    1 strip, ¼" × 6¼"
    1 strip, ¼" × 7"
    1 strip, ¼" × 7¾"
    (1 strip is untrimmed.)

From the Parchment wool, cut:
6 tulips

Appliquéing the Pillow Top

1. Arrange the stems on the Tobacco wool. Bunch the bottom ends near the bottom of the Tobacco wool in the following order, from left to right: 6¼", 7", 8", 5½", 7¾", and 6". Notice that the stems aren't positioned exactly side by side; you can overlap and bend them as desired, referring to the photo on page 12 and the diagram at right. Pin the stems in place.

2. Arrange the tulips, placing one atop each stem so that the bottom of the tulip overlaps the stem slightly. Pin in place.

3. Using Summer Brown or coordinating thread and a hand-sewing needle, whipstitch the stems and tulips in place.

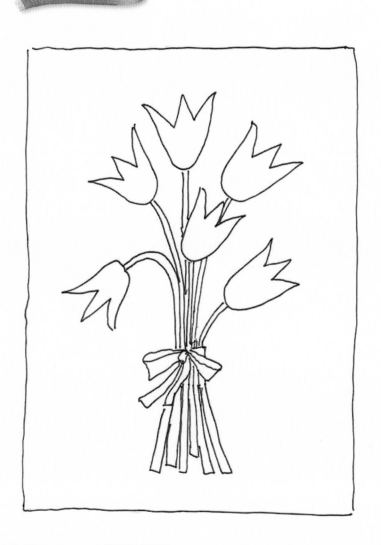

Assembling the Pillow

1. Place the pillow front and back right sides together and stitch using a ¼" seam allowance. Leave a 6" opening at the bottom.

Leave 6" opening.

2. Turn the pillow right side out and stuff. Hand stitch the opening closed.

3. Cut the length of ribbon in half. Turn under one end of one piece and hand stitch it to one side of the bunch of stems. Repeat using the other piece of ribbon on the other side of the bunch. Tie the pieces together in a bow.

Instant Vintage

If you dampen your ribbon with a little water and flatten it, it will appear aged.

Tulip

Early Radish and Sweet Peas

Radishes picked fresh from the garden—washed, with the leaves still attached—look so sweet and pair perfectly with a pod of sweet peas. Spring at its best.

FINISHED SCISSOR POCKET: 2¾" × 8"

FINISHED PIN KEEP: 1" × 5½"

Materials

I used wool from Blackberry Primitives (see "Resources" on page 95). To help you re-create this project, the materials list gives the exact color names for the wool I used.

- 5" × 6" piece of Red Velvet wool for radish
- 6" × 8" piece of Parchment wool for radish lining and top
- 3" × 8" piece of Army Green wool for radish leaves, pea pod cap, and tendril
- 4" × 7" piece of Pear wool for pea pod
- 9 assorted buttons, ¼" to ½" diameter, for pea pod and radish top
- Ground walnut shells or cotton stuffing for pea pod
- Hand-sewing supplies (see page 93)
- Freezer paper for transferring patterns

Cutting

Referring to "Wool Techniques" on page 93, use freezer paper and the patterns on page 20 to trace and then cut the radish and pea pod pieces.

From the Red Velvet wool, cut:
2 radishes

From the Parchment wool, cut:
2 radish linings
4 radish tops

From the Army Green wool, cut:
6 radish leaves
1 strip, ⅛" × 5"
1 pea pod cap

From the Pear wool, cut:
2 pea pods

*Radishes gathered in plump bunches,
so tempting they are eaten with
warm earth still clinging to them…*

~Sara Midda, In and Out of the Garden

Assembling the Radish Scissor Pocket

1. Layer each radish piece with a radish lining to create two sets, wrong sides together. Using Summer Brown or coordinating thread and a hand-sewing needle, whipstitch each set together along the top straight edge only.

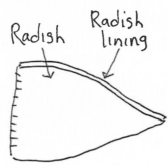

Radish   Radish lining

Make 2 sets.
Whipstitch straight edge only.

2. Layer the two sets with linings together. Whipstitch around the curved sides; leave the top open to create a pocket.

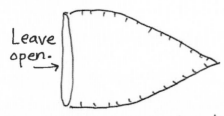

Leave open.

Layer 2 sets and whipstitch around curved sides.

3. Layer the radish tops in sets of two. For the radish-top front, whipstitch around the curved edge only; leave the bottom open. To make the buttonhole, center and cut a vertical slit through both layers, starting about ½" from the upper edge of the curve and making the slit about ⅛" larger than the button; be sure to use very sharp, pointed scissors. Buttonhole stitch (see page 95) around the raw edges of the buttonhole to prevent raveling.

4. For the radish-top back, whipstitch about 1" along the curve on each side, starting at the straight edge. Leave the bottom and the very top open (to allow for inserting the leaves). Layer the leaves in sets of two and whipstitch all the way around. Tuck the three leaves into the open seam of the radish-top back; whipstitch in place along the curved edge.

Radish-top back

Insert 3 leaves into the radish-top back and whipstitch in place.

5. Sew the radish-top front to one side of the radish pocket along the top edge, being sure to catch both of the pocket's fabric layers as you stitch. Repeat for the radish-top back.

6. Mark the button placement on the inside of the radish-top back. Sew on the button. Then tuck in your favorite embroidery scissors and button the pocket closed.

Assembling the Pea Pod Pin Keep

1. Stitch the pea pod pieces together along the curved edges using a running stitch and a ⅛" seam allowance. Gently turn right side out.

2. Stuff. If using ground walnut shells for stuffing, turn in the raw edges and stitch the pea pod partially closed to help contain the shells when filling. Add the shells until full, and then whipstitch the opening closed. If using cotton stuffing, it's easier to stuff the pea pod first and then turn in the raw edges and whipstitch closed.

3. Position and pin the Army Green ⅛" × 5" wool strip to the side of the pea pod, curving and looping the strip to create a tendril; whipstitch in place. Refer to the illustration above right and the photo on page 16 for placement.

4. Fold the pea pod cap over the end of the pea pod and whipstitch along the straight edges, attaching the cap to the pea pod as you stitch. Leave the cap points unstitched.

Fold.

Stitch this edge. Tendril and Cap placement

5. Sew buttons in graduated sizes to the side of the pea pod for peas.

Fashion a Chatelaine

You may have seen sewing chatelaines in museums or catalogs. Usually, they feature scissors in a sheath along with a thimble, attached to each other by a ribbon worn around the neck to keep sewing tools handy. To make the Early Radish and Sweet Peas into a chatelaine, cut a 1-yard length of primitive-looking (and soft) ribbon and stitch the radish on one end and the pea pod on the other. Drape the chatelaine ribbon around your neck—your tools will be right where you need them as you stitch! Cute (and easy).

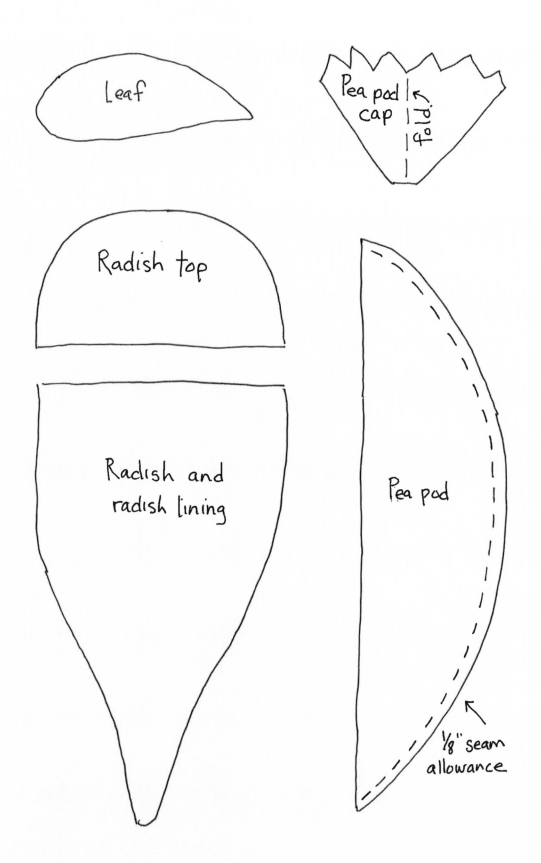

Leaf

Pea pod cap

fold

Radish top

Radish and radish lining

Pea pod

1/8" seam allowance

May Basket

In the past, May Day was celebrated by making sweet little baskets to give in secret. You'd fill a basket with flowers and candy, hang one on a doorknob or set it by a door, ring the doorbell, and run off before the door opened. Every day can be May Day with this cute little pin keep!

FINISHED PIN KEEP: 6" × 6"

Materials

I used wool from Blackberry Primitives (see "Resources" on page 95). To help you re-create this project, the materials list gives the exact color names for the wool I used.

- 6½" × 6½" square of Parchment wool for front
- 6½" × 6½" square of light-colored cotton for back
- 1¼" × 6½" piece of Ivory wool for basket, handle, and daisy
- 4 celluloid or bone buttons, ½" diameter, for flower centers
- Cotton stuffing
- Small scrap of old book page for starflower
- Hand-sewing supplies (see page 93)
- Freezer paper for transferring patterns

Cutting

Referring to "Wool Techniques" on page 93, use freezer paper and the patterns on page 23 to trace and then cut the appliqués.

From the Ivory wool, cut:
1 strip, ¼" × 6½"
1 strip, 1" × 4"
1 daisy

From the book page, cut:
1 starflower

Appliquéing the Pin Keep

1. Trace the triangle cutting pattern on page 23 onto the uncoated side of a piece of freezer paper. Press the waxy side of the freezer-paper strip to the right side of the Ivory wool 1" × 4" strip using the wool setting on the iron (no steam). Cut out the seven triangles on the traced lines and remove the freezer paper. Arrange the triangles on the Parchment wool to make a basket shape, with five triangles forming the basket and two triangles creating the basket feet; refer to the photo on page 22 for placement guidance. Pin in place.

2. Using Summer Brown or coordinating thread and a hand-sewing needle, whipstitch the triangles in place.

3. Position the ends of the ¼" × 6½" handle strip so they abut against the top basket triangles, about ¼" from the triangles' outer points. Create a smooth arc with the strip; pin and then whipstitch in place.

4. Layer one button over the daisy and sew it above the basket. Layer another button over the paper starflower and sew it near the handle. Sew on the two remaining buttons.

Finishing the Pin Keep

1. With right sides together, layer the pin keep front and cotton back. Stitch ¼" seams on all four sides, leaving a 3" opening along the bottom edge.

2. Turn the pin keep right side out. Fold in the raw edges of the opening, fill with cotton stuffing, and whipstitch the opening closed.

Explore Your Stash

This project can be an excuse to use some of your favorite old buttons. You may even have a few flower-shaped buttons in your button box. Embellish the basket as you wish and then add a bit of ribbon tied in a bow to the basket handle. What a great way to share some of your grandmother's buttons with family members!

Leave 3" opening.

Starflower

Daisy

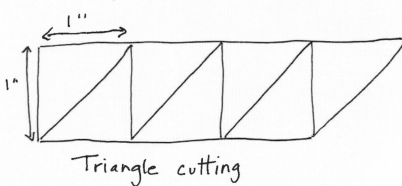

Triangle cutting

Potted Topiary

I love topiaries but have been unsuccessful in keeping them alive. Fortunately, I have found wonderful artificial ones, like this pillow. Make a topiary that doesn't need careful tending.

FINISHED PILLOW: 7½" × 14½"

Materials

I used wool from Blackberry Primitives (see "Resources" on page 95). To help you re-create this project, the materials list gives the exact color names for the wool I used.

- 8" × 15" piece of cream linen for pillow front*
- 8" × 15" piece of dark-colored cotton for pillow back
- 4" × 5" piece of Terra Cotta wool for flowerpot and rim
- 4" × 7" piece of Pear wool for leaves and grass in flowerpot
- 5" × 5" square of Army Green wool for letters
- ¼" × 6" strip of Hickory wool for tree trunk
- Small twig, about ⅛" × 5", for tree stake
- Cotton stuffing
- Hand-sewing supplies (see page 93)
- Freezer paper for transferring patterns
- Glue stick

You could also use matka silk, wool, or cotton.

Cutting

Referring to "Wool Techniques" on page 93, use the freezer paper and patterns on page 27 to trace and then cut the appliqués.

From the Terra Cotta wool, cut:
1 flowerpot
1 rim

From the Pear wool, cut:
1 grass filler
16 leaves

From the Army Green, cut:
Letters for *Topiary*

More Is Better

This could be a framed piece instead of a pillow. Topiaries are always better in groups! Create a runner with three topiaries along a length of fabric, omitting the word topiary.

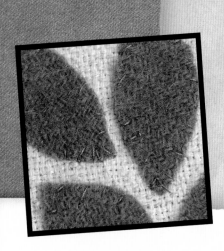

*Behind green clipped hedges tower
the shapes of the fantasy garden,
where since Roman times man has used
nature to fit his imagination.*

~Sara Midda, In and Out of the Garden

Appliquéing the Pillow Front

1. Center the flowerpot 1" above the bottom edge of the pillow front and pin in place; refer to the photo on page 24 for placement guidance. Using Summer Brown or coordinating thread and a hand-sewing needle, whipstitch in place.

2. Arrange the grass filler and then the rim at the top of the flowerpot, adjusting the placement to create a natural look with the grass filler tucked behind the rim. Pin; whipstitch in place.

3. Position the tree trunk at the top of the grass filler and pin with the bottom end tucked below the grass; notice that the trunk isn't perfectly straight to reflect natural growth. Whipstitch the trunk in place.

4. Arrange the 16 leaves above the tree trunk using the leaf placement diagram for guidance. Pin, and then whipstitch in place.

leaf placement

5. Apply a dab of glue stick on the wrong size of each letter, then arrange the letters. Whipstitch in place.

Assembling the Pillow

1. With right sides together and using a ¼" seam allowance, sew the pillow front and back together, leaving a 3" opening at the bottom. Turn right side out and fill with cotton stuffing. Turn in the raw edges along the opening and whipstitch closed.

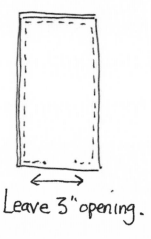

Leave 3" opening.

2. Position the twig next to the tree trunk. Using doubled thread, tie the stake to the trunk at three spots, leaving the thread ends loose as an accent.

Grass filler

Rim

Flowerpot

Leaf

Topiary

Step into My Garden

Sometimes you just can't stop at one—one stitch, one wool stack, one project! Here are three of my beloved garden blocks, featuring some of my favorite flowers and garden visitors. You can make each block as a stand-alone wall hanging, pillow, or framed piece of art—or assemble all three blocks as a table runner or bench seat by whipstitching them together.

FINISHED RUNNER SIZE: 14" × 40"

SNAIL BLOCK

FINISHED BLOCK: 14" × 16"

Materials

I used wool from Blackberry Primitives (see "Resources" on page 95). To help you re-create this project, the materials list gives the exact color names for the wool I used.

- 14" × 16" piece of Mudslide wool for background
- 6" × 16" piece of Pear wool for grass, stems, leaves, flower bases, and bud base
- ½" × 3½" strip of Army Green wool for leaf veins
- 2" × 6" piece of Red Velvet wool for flowers and bud
- 3" × 4" piece of Hazelnut wool for snail shell and dragonfly body
- 1" × 3" piece of Hickory wool for snail head, tail, and antennae
- 2" × 2" square of Parchment wool for dragonfly wings
- Hand-sewing supplies (see page 93)
- Freezer paper for transferring patterns

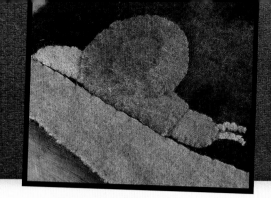

Cutting

Referring to "Wool Techniques" on page 93, use freezer paper, the patterns on pages 38–40 , and the cutting guide below to trace and cut the appliqués.

From the Pear wool, *first* cut:
1 grass A
1 strip, ¼" × 8"
1 strip, ¼" × 8½"
1 strip, ¼" × 9"

From the Pear wool, *next* cut:
3 A leaves
1 B leaf
1 C leaf
2 D leaves
2 E leaves
2 flower bases
1 bud base

From the Army Green wool, cut:
4 strips, ⅛" × 3½"

From the Red Velvet wool, use the cutting guide below to cut:
8 flower petals
1 bud

From the Hazelnut wool, cut:
1 snail shell
1 dragonfly body

From the Hickory wool, cut:
1 snail head
1 snail tail
2 snail antennae

From the Parchment wool, cut:
4 dragonfly wings

Appliquéing the Block

1. Position the grass at the bottom of the background and pin in place. Using Summer Brown or coordinating thread and a hand-sewing needle, whipstitch around all four sides.

2. Arrange and pin the three Pear strip stems and leaves A, B, and C at the top of the grass, overlapping and bending them as desired; refer to the photo on page 29 and the appliqué placement diagram for guidance. Whipstitch in place.

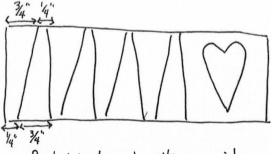

Red Velvet wool cutting guide

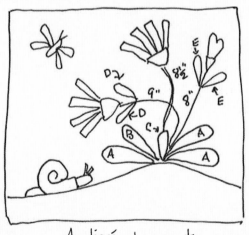

Appliqué placement

I know a little garden-close
set thick with lily and red rose,
where I would wander if I might
from dewy dawn to dewy night
~William Morris

3. Position the four Army Green strips on the A and B leaves, trimming the length as desired. Pin and then whipstitch in place.

4. Position two D leaves, two E leaves, two flower bases, and one bud base; pin. Whipstitch in place, leaving the straight edges of the three bases open.

5. Tuck the flower petals and the bud into the top of the flower and bud bases. Pin and then whipstitch in place.

6. Position the snail shell, tail, head, and antennae; pin and then whipstitch in place. Position the dragonfly body and wings, tucking the wings under the body; pin and then whipstitch in place.

7. To add accent stitching, use a running stitch to create the snail coil; see page 39. Add two straight stitches for dragonfly antennae.

Success with Small Appliqués

If you're working with teeny pieces, like the snail antennae, or very narrow strips, like the ⅛"-wide leaf veins you may find that the pieces unravel a bit as you try to whipstitch the edges—especially if you're working with loosely woven wool. If the small whipstitch unravels the tiny pieces of wool, couch them in place by stitching over the narrow pieces instead of stitching through them, anchoring them to the background (see page 95). Wool is very forgiving! You can also continue to take tiny whipstitches, catching all the loose fibers as you stitch. If a narrow strip unravels or tears apart completely, simply overlap the two edges, take super teeny stitches to rejoin the strip, and continue whipstitching. Of course, if your damaged piece no longer fits the space, perhaps you can adapt your design slightly or cut a new piece.

BEE SKEP BLOCK

FINISHED BLOCK: 12" × 14"

Materials

I used wool from Blackberry Primitives (see "Resources" on page 95). To help you re-create this project, the materials list gives the exact color names for the wool I used.

- 12" × 14" piece of Mudslide wool *OR* 2 pieces of Mudslide wool, 7½" × 14" and 5" × 14" (see "Piecing the Background," right)

- 4" × 12" piece of Pear windowpane wool* for grass and leaves

- 6" × 9" piece of Squash wool for bee skep

- 2" × 4" piece of Tobacco wool for skep door and flower centers

- 2" × 11½" piece of Pear solid wool for stems, tendril, and leaves

- 2½" × 5½" piece of Red Velvet wool for flowers

- 1" × 2" piece of black-and-white tweed or herringbone wool for bees

- 1" × 2" piece of Parchment wool for bee wings

- Hand-sewing supplies (see page 93)

- Freezer paper for transferring patterns

*This is a windowpane-plaid piece of wool that's been dyed the Pear color; the subtle plaid adds texture.

Piecing the Background

To add interest, I pieced the background of my Bee Skep block using two pieces of Mudslide wool with different values (one piece is dyed darker than the other; this is a naturally occurring difference in the dyeing process). If you'd like to piece your background, purchase two pieces of wool, overlap one piece with the other by ½", and whipstitch the edge; this makes a nice flat seam. Check your block width to be sure it is 12" wide.

Cutting

Referring to "Wool Techniques" on page 93, use freezer paper and the patterns on pages 38–40 to trace and then cut the appliqués.

From the Pear windowpane wool, *first* cut:
1 grass B

From the Pear windowpane wool, *next* cut:
2 G leaves
1 H leaf
6 I leaves

From the Squash wool, cut:
1 bee skep

From the Tobacco wool, cut:
1 skep door
10 flower centers

From the Pear solid wool, cut:
1 strip, ⅛" × 11"
1 strip, ¼" × 9"
1 strip, ¼" × 10"
1 strip, ¼" × 11"
1 F leaf
2 G leaves
1 H leaf

From the Red Velvet wool, cut:
10 flowers

From the black-and-white tweed, cut:
3 bees

From the Parchment wool, cut:
6 bee wings

Appliquéing the Block

1. Position the grass at the bottom of the background and pin in place. Using Summer Brown or coordinating thread and a hand-sewing needle, whipstitch around the two sides and bottom.

2. Tuck the bee skep under the grass, trimming to reduce bulk if necessary. Pin and then whipstitch the skep in place. Position the bee skep door; pin. Whipstitch in place.

3. Use a running stitch to designate the bee skep coils; refer to the photo on page 32 for guidance.

4. Referring to the diagram on page 34, position and pin two ¼"-wide Pear strips for stems, the ⅛"-wide Pear strip for tendril, and the leaves on the right side of the skep, tucking them under the grass and trimming to reduce bulk if necessary. Taper the upper end of the tendril. Whipstitch in place.

5. Arrange the remaining stem and leaves on the left side of the skep; pin and then whipstitch in place. Whipstitch the top edge of the grass in place over the appliqués.

Help with Stems and Tendrils

Tendrils are a favorite element in my appliqué. The wool must be thin to twist and turn, just as a tendril does in nature, with the end tapering to a point. I have found an easy way to stitch these narrow pieces that works well on stems less than ½" wide. Instead of stitching up one side and then down the other, you stitch both sides alternately. Work from the bottom of the stem or tendril up to the tip, taking one stitch and then passing underneath the appliqué to re-emerge on the other side and take another stitch.

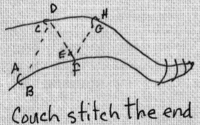

Couch stitch the end of the stem or tendril.

6. Position the flowers and flower centers along the stems; pin and then whipstitch in place. Arrange the bees and bee wings, tucking the wings under the bees; pin and whipstitch in place.

Appliqué Placement

Make a Beeline

For a little extra decoration on this block, create a running stitch "flight" pattern for the bee on the left, curving the running stitches up and over the middle flower and looping it once as you approach the bee.

STEP INTO MY GARDEN BLOCK

FINISHED BLOCK: 12" × 14"

Materials

I used wool from Blackberry Primitives (see "Resources" on page 95). To help you re-create this project, the materials list gives the exact color names for the wool I used.

- 12" × 14" piece of Mudslide wool for background
- 7" × 12" piece of Pear wool for grass, stems, leaves, and flower bases
- 3" × 3½" piece of Red Velvet wool for petals
- 8" × 12" piece of Hickory wool for letters
- ½" × 2" piece of Hazelnut wool for dragonfly
- 1" × 3" piece of Parchment wool for dragonfly wings
- Hand-sewing supplies (see page 93)
- Freezer paper for transferring patterns
- Glue stick

Cutting

Referring to "Wool Techniques" on page 93, use freezer paper and the patterns on pages 38, 39, 41, and 42 to trace and then cut the appliqués.

From the Pear wool, *first* cut:
1 grass C

From the Pear wool, *next* cut:
4 strips, ¼" × 12"; crosscut into:
    2 strips, ¼" × 10"
    1 strip, ¼" × 8¾"
    1 strip, ¼" × 7"
2 J leaves
4 K leaves
2 L leaves
2 M leaves
5 N leaves
4 flower bases

From the Hickory wool, cut:
Step into my Garden letters

Continued on page 36

Continued from page 35

From the Red Velvet wool, cut:

1 strip, 1¾" × 3"

1 strip, 1¼" × 3"

Use these strips and the cutting guides below to cut 7 flower 1 petals and 6 flower 2 petals.

From the Hazelnut wool, cut:

1 dragonfly body

From the Parchment wool, cut:

4 dragonfly wings

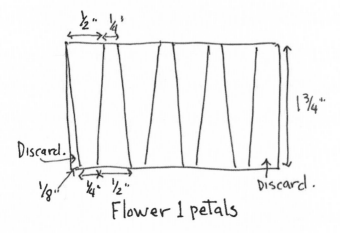

Flower 1 petals

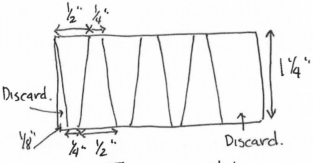

Flower 2 petals

Red Velvet wool cutting guide

Appliquéing the Block

1. Position the grass at the bottom of the background and pin in place. Using Summer Brown or coordinating thread and a hand-sewing needle, whipstitch around all four sides.

2. Arrange and pin the stems and leaves, overlapping and bending them as desired; refer to the diagram on page 37 and the photo on page 35 for guidance. Whipstitch in place.

3. Position the four flower bases; pin and then whipstitch the curved edges in place, leaving the straight edges open. Reserve the flower petals for flower 2 on the left until after the letters are stitched. Tuck the remaining flower petals into the top of three flower bases; pin and then whipstitch in place.

4. Apply a dab of glue stick on the wrong side of each letter to hold it in place as you position and pin it, overlapping the stems and leaves as shown in the appliqué placement diagram. Whipstitch in place.

5. Position the flower petals for the remaining flower (placing one or two petals over the letter *S*) and pin; whipstitch in place.

6. Position the dragonfly body and wings, tucking the wings under the body; pin and whipstitch in place. If desired, add two straight stitches for dragonfly antennae.

Appliqué placement

Find Your "Wool" Voice

This block invites creativity—and your favorite phrase! Ponder all the possibilities (those that will fit, of course), whether the words are from a famous passage, consist of a list of your favorite flowers, or are simple words to live by. Enlarge the appliqué placement diagram (the outlines will be fuzzy at a large size), then tape tracing paper over the diagram. Try sketching different words and word placements and changing the position of the stems and flowers to show off your new design. Let your imagination soar!

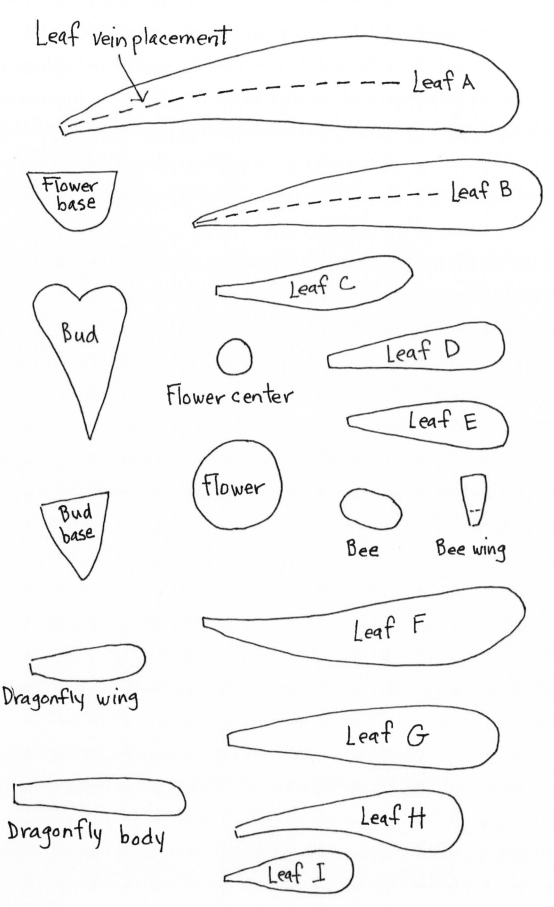

Leaf vein placement

Leaf A

Flower base

Leaf B

Bud

Leaf C

Flower center

Leaf D

Leaf E

Flower

Bud base

Bee

Bee wing

Leaf F

Dragonfly wing

Leaf G

Dragonfly body

Leaf H

Leaf I

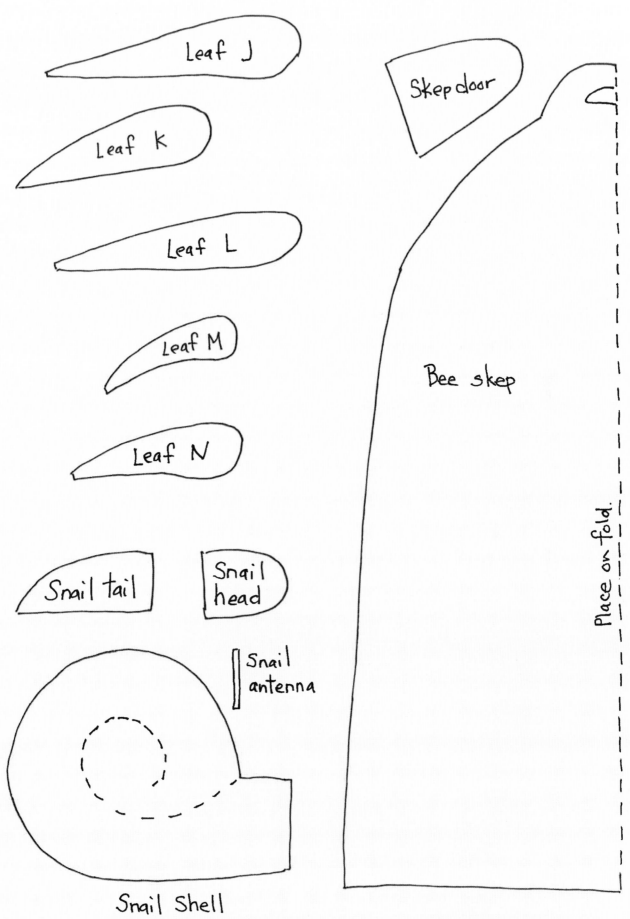

Leaf J

Leaf K

Leaf L

Leaf M

Leaf N

Skep door

Bee skep

Place on fold.

Snail tail

Snail head

Snail antenna

Snail Shell

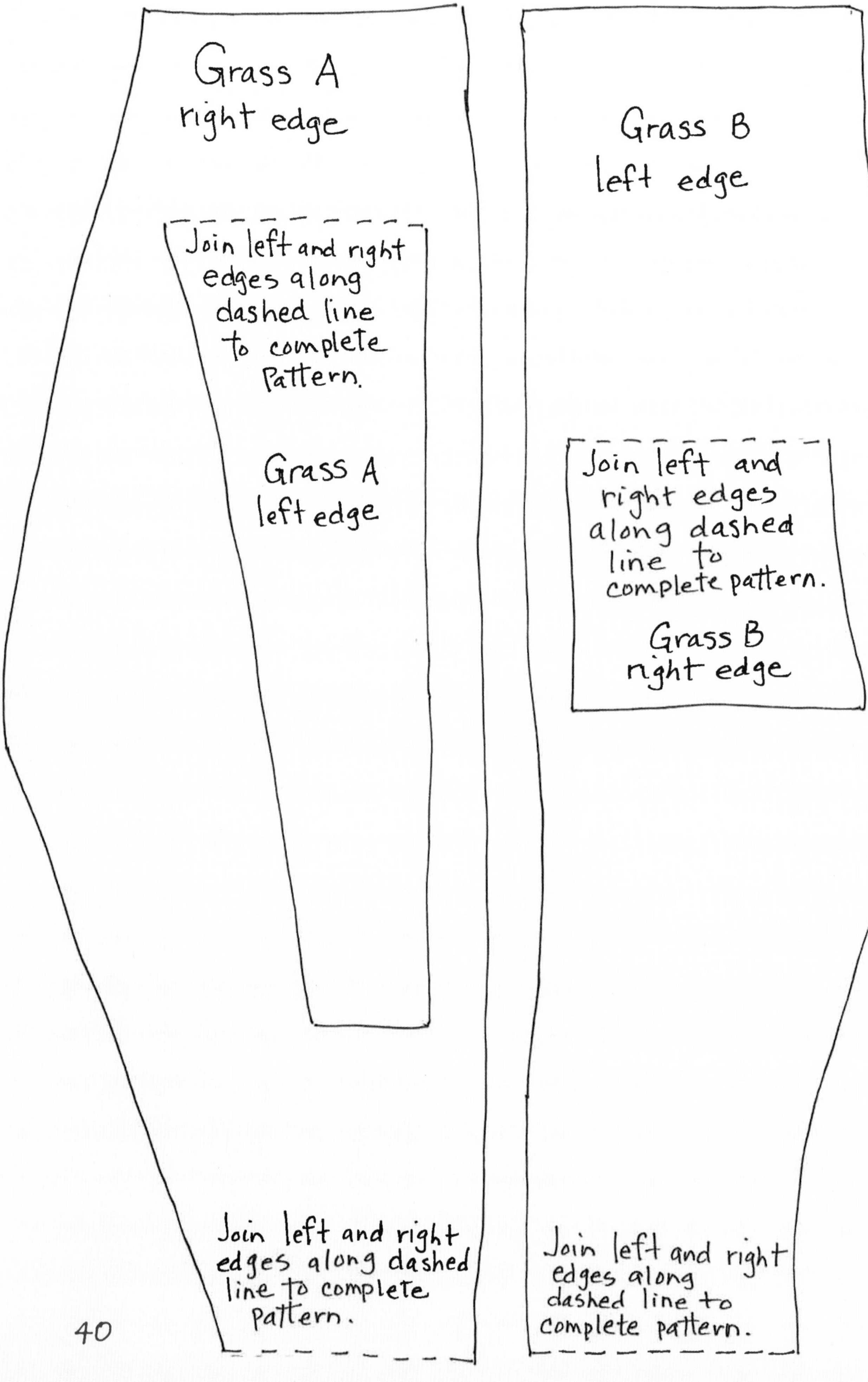

Grass A
right edge

Join left and right
edges along
dashed line
to complete
Pattern.

Grass A
left edge

Grass B
left edge

Join left and
right edges
along dashed
line to
complete pattern.

Grass B
right edge

Join left and right
edges along dashed
line to complete
Pattern.

Join left and right
edges along
dashed line to
complete pattern.

Join left and right edges along dashed line to complete pattern.

Grass C
right edge

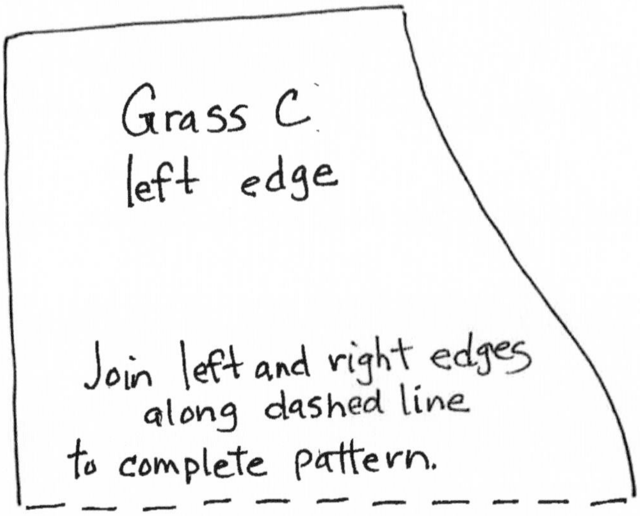

Grass C
left edge

Join left and right edges along dashed line to complete pattern.

Strawberry Fields

Strawberries can be made from an assortment of fabrics. Making a bowlful will create a colorful centerpiece—it's a great way to display fabrics, as well as buttons, from your collection. Strawberries filled with emery sand will remove oxidation from your sewing needles, so keep your sweet strawberries handy when you're stitching.

FINISHED STRAWBERRY PIN KEEP: 5½" high

Materials

I used wool and velvet from Blackberry Primitives (see "Resources" on page 95). To help you re-create this project, the materials list gives the exact color names for the wool I used.

- 7" × 11" piece of soft red velvet, wool, or cotton for strawberry
- 4" × 4½" piece of Pear wool for cap and stem
- Cotton stuffing, ground walnut shells, or emery sand
- Hand-sewing supplies (see page 93)
- Freezer paper for transferring patterns
- 12 two-hole pearl or shell buttons, ⅜" diameter, for seeds

Cutting

Referring to "Wool Techniques" on page 93, use freezer paper and the patterns on page 47 to trace and then cut the strawberry and cap.

From the red velvet, cut:
1 strawberry*

From the Pear wool, cut:
1 strawberry cap
1 strip, 1" × 2½"

*See "Cutting Velvet" on page 45.

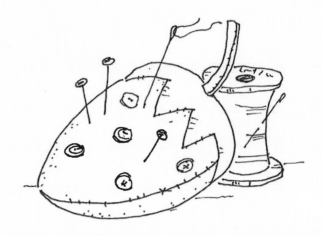

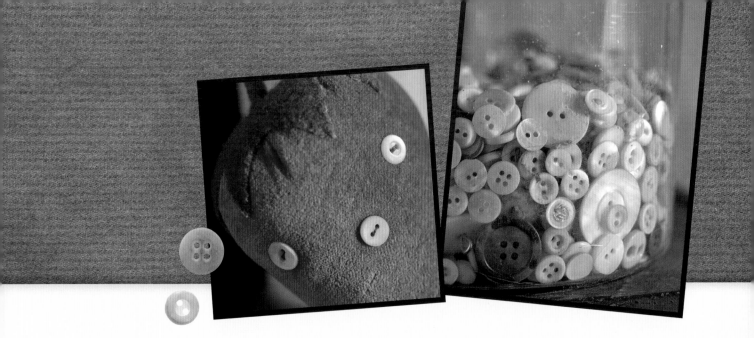

Cutting Velvet

Even though the pattern for the strawberry shows a fold line, if you're using velvet it's best to cut it in a single layer. Velvet has a nap that tends to make the fabric shift when you cut a double layer. You'll need to have a full paper pattern for a single-layer cut. The easiest way to create a full pattern is to make two photocopies of page 47, cut out the patterns just outside the lines, and tape them together (one right side up, one wrong side up and matching the fold lines exactly). Hold the taped pattern up to a window and draw the wrong side pattern line on the right side of your paper to create a full pattern. Place the full pattern on a single layer of velvet, pin in place, and cut the strawberry.

Making the Pin Keep

1. Fold the strawberry velvet in half with right sides together. Referring to the pattern on page 47, sew the side seam and around the lower curve using Summer Brown or coordinating thread and a ¼" seam allowance. Leave the top edge open. Turn right side out and stuff firmly and evenly with your choice of stuffing.

2. With doubled thread, make two rows of gathering stitches around the top edge; pull gently to draw the opening closed. Knot the thread securely.

3. Place the strawberry cap on top of the gathered area. Whipstitch the cap in place, spacing and smoothing the points as you stitch; see the photo on page 44 for placement guidance.

4. Lay the Pear wool strip flat, then roll it tightly lengthwise to create a stem. Whipstitch along the length of the raw edge to prevent it from unrolling.

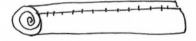

5. Place the stem at the center of the strawberry cap, stitch the lower edge in place, and knot securely.

Stitch.

Make an Emery Bag

You can buy emery sand online and use it to stuff your strawberry. Jab pins and needles into the emery bag to remove oxidation and make them smooth again.

6. Sew the buttons onto the strawberry for seeds.

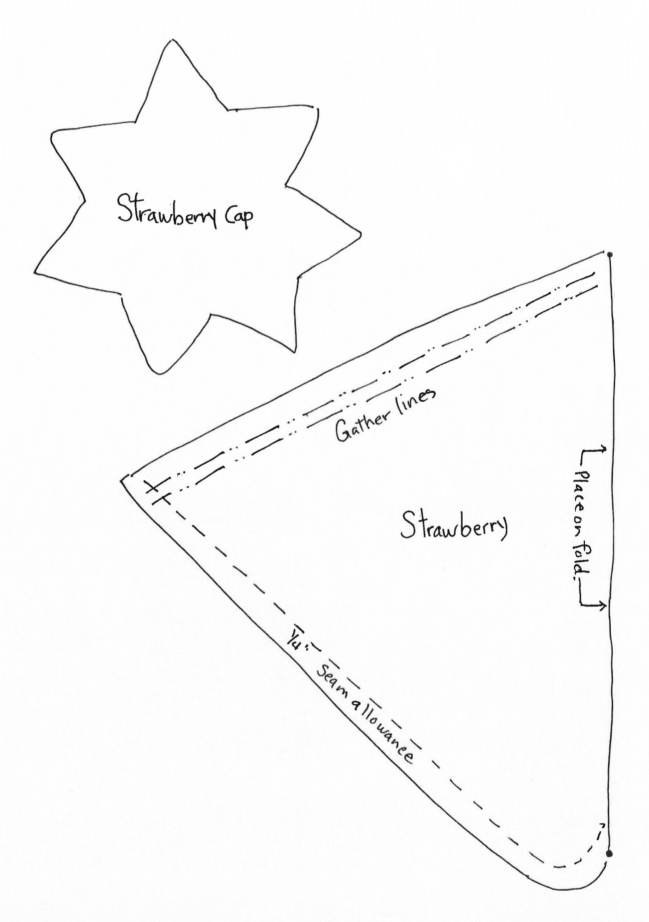

Strawberry Cap

Gather lines

Strawberry

Place on fold.

1/4" Seam allowance

Slice o' Summer

Anything better than an ice-cold slice of watermelon on a steamy summer day? Nothing that I can think of! This summery pin keep will stitch up quickly—a perfect project while you're relaxing on the patio.

FINISHED PIN KEEP: 4" × 5½"

Materials

I used wool from Blackberry Primitives (see "Resources" on page 95). To help you re-create this project, the materials list gives the exact color names for the wool I used.

- 6" × 10" piece of coarse natural cotton for front and back
- 4" × 5¼" piece of Red Velvet wool for melon
- ½" × 10" strip of Ivory wool for rind
- ½" × 10" strip of Pear wool for rind
- 1" × 2" piece of Black wool for seeds
- Cotton stuffing
- ¾" × 2½" slip of paper
- 1 quilt pin, 1¾" long
- Hand-sewing supplies (see page 93)
- Freezer paper for transferring patterns
- Pigma Micron 03 (.35 mm) permanent black ink pen

Cutting

Referring to "Wool Techniques" on page 93, use freezer paper and the patterns on page 51 to trace and then cut the appliqués.

From the Red Velvet wool, cut:
1 melon

From the Black wool, cut:
5 seeds

Appliquéing the Pin Keep

1. Fold the cotton in half crosswise with wrong sides together to create a 5" × 6" rectangle.

2. Center the melon ¾" above the fold, then pin in place through one layer of fabric. Notice I placed my melon at an angle. Unfold the cotton for stitching.

3. Using Summer Brown or coordinating thread and a hand-sewing needle, whipstitch the melon in place.

4. Place the Ivory strip so that one long edge sits along and covers the outer melon edge and pin in place. Trim the rind even with the upper edges of the melon. Whipstitch in place.

49

5. Cut one long edge of the Pear strip in an irregular scallop, and then place this edge over the Ivory rind; trim both short ends of the strip so they're even with the rind and melon. Whipstitch in place.

6. Arrange the seeds on the melon. Pin and whipstitch in place.

Finishing the Pin Keep

1. Fold the cotton rectangle in half again with right sides together. Stitch ¼" seams on both sides, but do not turn the pin keep right side out.

2. To make a box corner so the pin keep sits upright, square off one bottom corner by bringing the imaginary bottom "fold line" together with a side seam. Press flat and pin. Measure in ½" from the corner and draw a line perpendicular to the seams as shown. Stitch along this line. Repeat for the other corner.

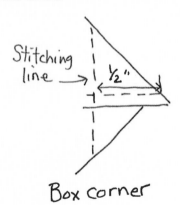

Box corner

3. Turn the pin keep right side out. Fold in the raw edges of the top opening, fill with cotton stuffing, and whipstitch the opening closed.

4. Using a window or light box and the *Watermelon* lettering on page 51, center and trace the letters on the slip of paper using the black pen. Use the quilt pin to attach it decoratively on the pin keep.

The Sweet Fruits of Summer

Need quick exchange gifts for your quilt guild or book club? With a fruitful imagination and a few color changes, this watermelon can become an orange or an apple. For an orange, make the outer rind a rich orange color and the inner background a lighter orange, and transform the seed shapes into large orange segments. For an apple, combine the rind pieces into one ruby red peel, make the background winter white, and scatter a few seeds closer to the center.

WATERMELON

⬭ Seed

Melon

Blossoming

This little pocket purse is perfect for taking to craft fairs, antique shows, or a day at the park. You'll have enough room to hold an ID and a credit card or some folded money. You can shop, eat, and visit with your hands free!

FINISHED PURSE: 3¼" × 4½"

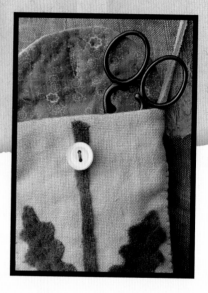

Materials

I used wool from Blackberry Primitives (see "Resources" on page 95). To help you re-create this project, the materials list gives the exact color names for the wool I used.

- 8" × 8" piece of natural linen for purse
- 8" × 8" piece of tan print cotton for lining
- 2" × 5" piece of Army Green wool for stem and leaves
- 2" × 3" piece of Waterfall wool for flower
- 1 button, ½" diameter
- 40" of natural leather cord
- Hand-sewing supplies (see page 93)
- Freezer paper for transferring patterns

Cutting

Referring to "Wool Techniques" on page 93, use freezer paper and the patterns on page 55 to trace and then cut the pocket and appliqués.

From the natural linen, cut:
1 pocket front
1 pocket back

From the tan print, cut:
1 pocket front
1 pocket back

From the Army Green wool, cut:
2 leaves
1 strip, ¼" × 5"; taper slightly toward one end

From the Waterfall wool, cut:
1 flower

Making the Purse

1. With right sides together, sew the linen and tan print pocket fronts together around the sides and top using a ¼" seam allowance; leave the bottom open. Turn right side out through the opening, fold in the raw edge, and whipstitch the opening closed. In the same manner, sew the linen and tan print pocket backs together, turn right side out, fold in the raw edge, and whipstitch closed.

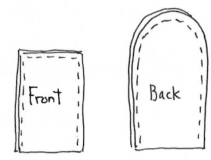

Leave bottoms open for turning.

2. Arrange the Army Green strip and two leaves on the front and pin in place using the photo on page 52 for placement. Using Summer Brown or coordinating thread and a hand-sewing needle, whipstitch in place.

3. Position the flower on the curved flap of the pocket back, pin, and whipstitch in place.

4. Use a running stitch to add petal lines to the flower and veins to the leaves; refer to the photo for guidance.

5. To make a buttonhole, center and cut a vertical slit in the pocket flap through all three layers, starting about ½" from the lower edge of the appliquéd flower and making the slit about ⅛" larger than the button; be sure to use very sharp, pointed scissors. Buttonhole stitch (see page 95) around the raw edges of the buttonhole to prevent raveling.

6. With wrong sides together, whipstitch the pocket front and back together along the sides and bottom, keeping the flap free. Reinforce the corners with extra stitching.

7. Make a knot at each end of the cording and stitch the ends to the inside of the purse at the side seams (see top-left photo on page 55).

8. Close the flap and mark the placement for the button. Sew the button to the pocket front, taking care not to catch the pocket back when stitching.

Phone Purse

This purse can be easily adapted to carry a cell phone; simply enlarge the pattern to fit your phone. The appliqué can remain the same size, but you may need to lengthen the stem. Be sure to choose a sturdy cord and attach it securely.

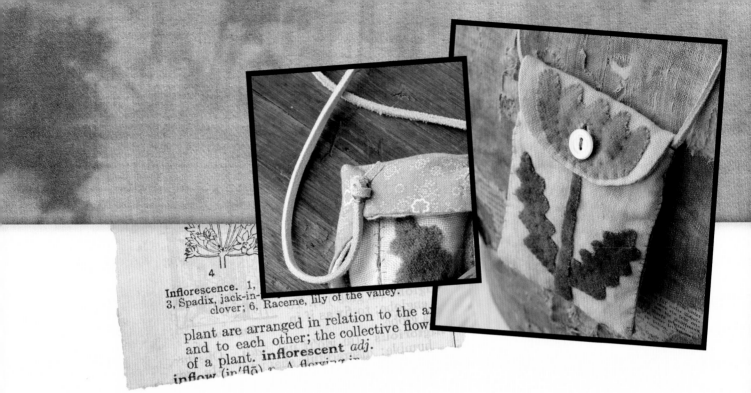

Flower

Leaf

Pocket front

Stitch line for front

Pocket back and flap

¼" Seam allowance

Tomato, Tomahto

You can never have too many tomato pincushions! Keep it classic with luscious reds, or take a cue from nature and grow your pincushion collection in an assortment of yellows, oranges, purples, and greens.

FINISHED PINCUSHIONS: approximately 5½", 4½", and 3¼" diameter

Materials

Yields 3 pincushions. I used wool and velvet from Blackberry Primitives (see "Resources" on page 95). To help you re-create this project, the materials list gives the exact color names for the wool I used.

- 7½" × 15" piece of red cotton print for large tomato
- 6" × 12" piece of Red Velvet wool for medium tomato
- 4½" × 9" piece of red velvet for small tomato
- 5" × 6" piece of Pear wool for blossom ends and stems
- 1¼" × 2" scrap of homespun cotton for large tomato patch
- Hand-sewing supplies (see page 93)
- Green embroidery floss (DMC 733)
- Large-eye needle for floss
- Cotton stuffing
- Freezer paper for transferring patterns

Cutting

Referring to "Wool Techniques" on page 93, use freezer paper and the patterns on page 59 to trace and then cut the appliqués.

From the red cotton, cut:
2 large tomatoes

From the Red Velvet wool, cut:
2 medium tomatoes

From the red velvet, cut:
2 small tomatoes

From the Pear wool, cut:
2 blossom ends
1 small blossom end
2 strips, 1½" × 2"
1 strip, 1" × 2"

Sewing the Pincushions

1. With right sides together, join the large cotton tomato shapes using a scant ¼" seam allowance and leaving a 2" opening. Turn the tomato right side out, stuff firmly, turn in the raw edges, and whipstitch closed. Repeat for the medium wool and small velvet tomatoes.

2. Stuff each tomato with cotton stuffing, arranging the tomato with the seam so it is horizontal around the widest part of the tomato.

3. Cut a length of six-stranded embroidery floss for each pincushion as follows: 3 yards for the large, 2½ yards for the medium, and 2 yards for the small.

4. Thread the needle with all six strands and knot the end of the floss multiple times. For each pincushion, insert the needle into the bottom center of the tomato and out the top center, pulling the knot inside (use the point of the needle to pull aside fabric fibers so the knot can pass through, if needed). Circle over the outside of the tomato and reinsert the needle and floss in the bottom center, pulling the floss taut to make an indentation. Repeat five times, spacing the floss indentations evenly around the tomato. Knot the floss securely at the center top of the pincushion; trim the end.

5. Using Summer Brown or coordinating thread, stitch a blossom end to the top of the large and medium tomatoes and a small blossom end to the small tomato, securing them in place with a few stitches and leaving the points loose.

6. Roll each Pear wool strip tightly lengthwise to create a stem. Whipstitch along the length of the raw edge to prevent it from unrolling. Using the larger stems for the medium and large tomatoes and the smaller stem for the small tomato, place a stem at the center of each blossom end, stitch the lower edges in place, and knot securely.

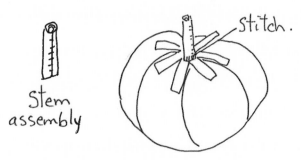

Stem assembly

Stitch.

7. Add a decorative patch to the large tomato by turning under the raw edges of the homespun scrap; press. Place the patch on the side of the tomato and whipstitch in place. If desired, create an X on the patch using a running stitch.

Who Wouldn't Love a Tomato Pillow?

Make a giant tomato pillow for daytime snoozing! Cut two 16" circles of soft fabric and follow the directions to sew, stuff, and accent your tomato. Use heavier-weight pearl cotton or yarn in place of floss to make the indentations.

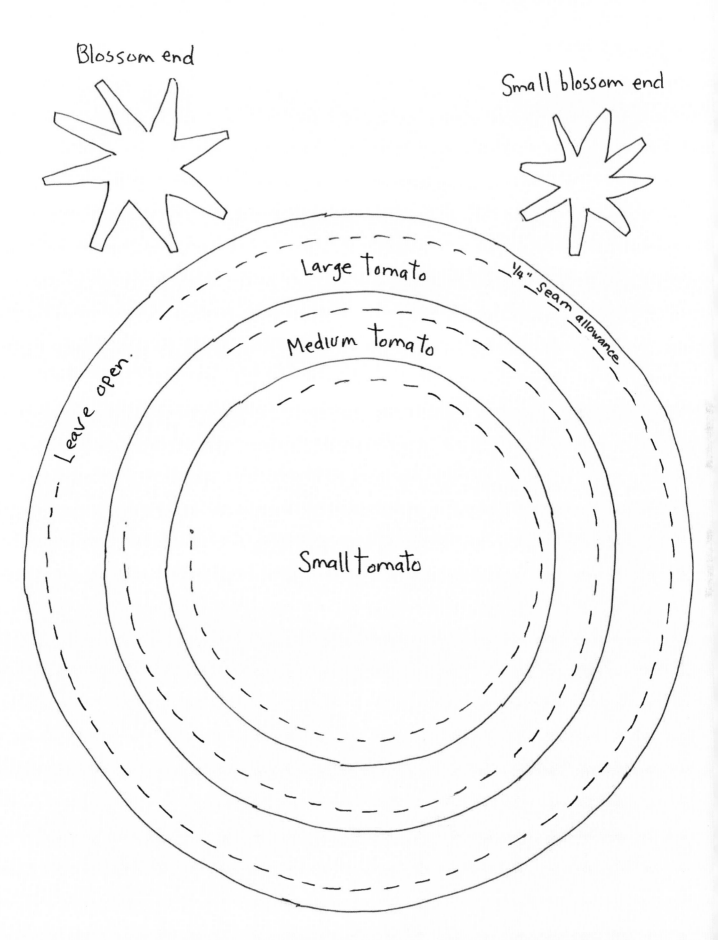

Blossom end

Small blossom end

Large Tomato

¼" seam allowance

Medium Tomato

Leave open.

Small Tomato

Sunshine on a Stem

Sunflowers are so cheerful, and I love to watch them follow the sun. They're like large solar disks. Finish this sunflower project as you wish; the bouquet can be a wall hanging, table mat, pillow, or framed art.

FINISHED WALL HANGING: 10" × 18"

Materials

I used wool from Blackberry Primitives (see "Resources" on page 95). To help you re-create this project, the materials list gives the exact color names for the wool I used.

- 10" × 18" piece of blue-and-white ticking for background*
- 3" × 14" piece of Pear wool for stems, leaves, and flower base
- 3" × 6" piece of Black wool for flower centers
- 4" × 9" piece of Mustard wool for large-flower and bent-flower petals
- 1" × 8¼" strip of Chestnut wool for middle-flower petals
- 1½" × 1½" square of black-and-brown tweed wool for seeds
- 2¾" × 4¾" piece of white muslin for label
- Hand-sewing supplies (see page 93)
- Pigma Micron 01 (.25 mm) permanent black ink pen
- Freezer paper for transferring patterns

*My piece of ticking has four raw, frayed edges—I love how it looks! If you prefer, turn back the raw edges and whipstitch to secure them. You could also use wool for the background.

Cutting

Referring to "Wool Techniques" on page 93, use freezer paper and the patterns on page 65 to trace and then cut the appliqués.

From the Pear wool, cut:
3 strips, ¼" × 14"; crosscut into:
    1 strip, ¼" × 14"
    1 strip, ¼" × 11½"
    1 strip, ¼" × 10"
1 A leaf
3 B leaves
1 C leaf
1 flower base

From the Black wool, cut:
1 large-flower center
1 middle-flower center

From the Mustard wool, cut:
1 strip, 1¾" × 9"
1 strip, 1" × 8"
1 strip, 1¼" × 2"
1 strip, ⅞" × 2"

From the tweed wool, cut:
6 seeds

*So always look for the silver lining
and try to find the sunny side of life.*
~Sir Pelham Grenville Wodehouse

Preparing the Petal Appliqués

For a more primitive look, you may cut the petals from the wool strips freehand; see "Freehand Cutting for Petals" at right. Or, if you prefer uniform petal shapes and sizes, follow these directions to use the patterns.

1. Trace the pattern (page 66) for the large flower's outer petals onto freezer paper, then press it lightly onto the Mustard 1¾" × 9" strip using the wool setting on your iron (no steam). Following the pattern lines, cut three-quarters of the way into the strip to create the outer petals, but leave the lower edge uncut so the strip stays together. Repeat with the Mustard 1" × 8" strip and the large flower's inner-petals pattern.

2. Using the freezer-paper technique, press the pattern for the bent flower's lower petals onto the Mustard 1¼" × 2" strip and cut the lower petals. Repeat for the mustard ⅞" × 2" strip and the bent flower's upper petals.

3. Use the Chestnut 1" × 8¼" strip and the middle flower's petals pattern to cut the petals for the middle flower using the freezer-paper technique.

Freehand Cutting for Petals

If you decide to cut the petals freehand, snip down only about three-quarters of the way to the lower edge of the strip to keep the strip intact. Use the following spacing between petal tips.

For the large flower's outer petals, use the Mustard 1¾" × 9" strip and cut 10 petals, approximately ⅞" apart.

For the large flower's inner petals, use the Mustard 1" × 8" strip and cut 13 petals, approximately ⅝" apart.

For the middle flower's petals, use the Chestnut 1" × 8¼" strip and cut 14 petals, approximately ½" to ⅝" apart.

For the bent flower's lower petals, use the Mustard 1¼" × 2" strip and cut three petals, approximately ⅝" apart.

For the bent flower's upper petals, use the Mustard ⅞" × 2" strip and cut four petals, approximately ½" apart.

Appliquéing the Wall Hanging

1. Referring to the diagram on page 64, arrange and pin the Pear strips on the ticking, placing them left to right in the following order: 14", 11½", and 10".

2. Using Summer Brown or coordinating thread and a hand-sewing needle, whipstitch the stems in place. Position the leaves on the stems, pin, and whipstitch in place.

3. Position the two flower centers and the flower base on the stems. Pin and whipstitch in place.

4. Position the uncut edge of the flower outer-petal strip around the large flower's center so that the edges align and the short ends of the strip meet; pin and whipstitch in place. Position the inner-petal strip on top of the flower center, just inside the outer-petals strip, gathering any excess as you whipstitch it in place.

5. Position the uncut edge of the middle flower's petal strip around the edge of the middle flower's center so the ends of the strip meet; pin and whipstitch in place.

6. Place the bent flower's lower-petal strip along the straight edge of the flower base. Pin and whipstitch in place. Place the upper-petal strip on top so it overlaps the base and whipstitch in place.

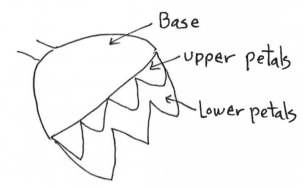

Bent-flower petal placement

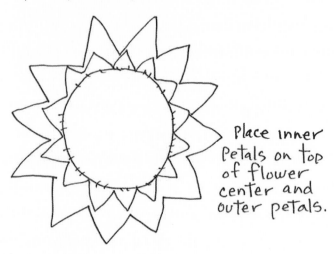

Place inner petals on top of flower center and outer petals.

Large-flower petal placement

7. Position three seeds in each open flower and whipstitch in place.

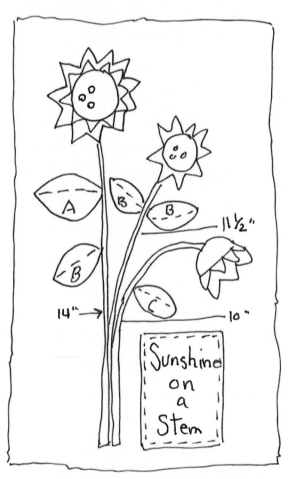

8. Use a running stitch to create veins in the leaves.

9. Using a window or light box and the black pen, center and trace the *Sunshine on a Stem* letters (page 65) on the muslin.

10. Attach the muslin label to the ticking using a running stitch, leaving the edges raw.

"I Must Have Flowers..."

"...Always, and always," said Claude Monet. This project is your opportunity to have any type of flower you desire. Try a thistle, daisy, or lady's slipper—or how about a daffodil, iris, or hollyhock? Just a quick online search for simple floral shapes that are in the public domain will yield a whole garden of upright and easy-to-draw flowers and leaves. Inspiration is all you need!

Sunshine on a Stem

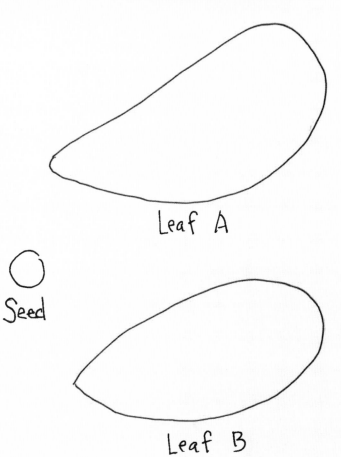

Leaf A

Leaf B

O Seed

Large-flower center

Middle-flower center

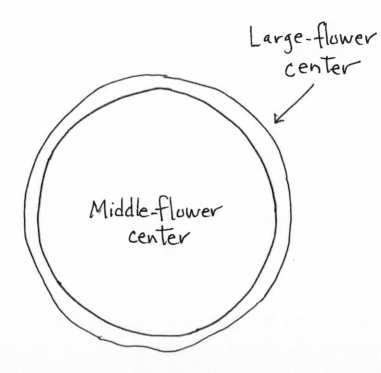

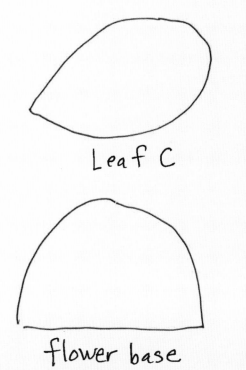

Leaf C

flower base

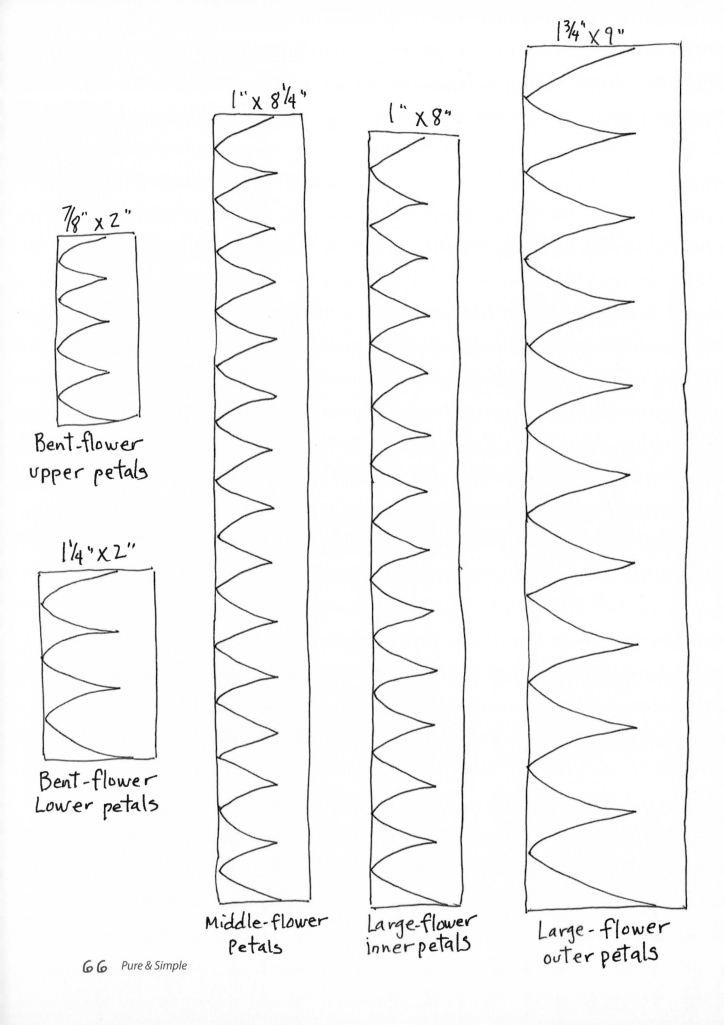

7/8" x 2"

Bent-flower
upper petals

1 1/4" x 2"

Bent-flower
Lower petals

1" x 8 1/4"

Middle-flower
Petals

1" x 8"

Large-flower
inner petals

1 3/4" x 9"

Large-flower
outer petals

Give Thanks

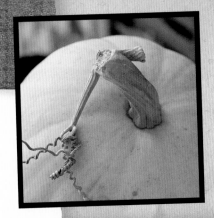

This Give Thanks project can be part of your decor all through the fall—it's a great sentiment. You certainly can change the colors if you prefer an orange pumpkin; just cut the berries from Parchment wool. You might re-create the appliqué design as your centerpiece by setting a pumpkin on a cake pedestal and tucking in real or artificial bittersweet berries.

FINISHED WALL HANGING: 14" × 15"

Materials

I used wool from Blackberry Primitives (see "Resources" on page 95). To help you re-create this project, the materials list gives the exact color names for the wool I used.

- 14" × 15" piece of Tobacco wool for background
- 5¼" × 10" piece of Old Ivory wool for pedestal top and base
- 6¼" × 8" piece of Parchment wool for pumpkin
- 5" × 15" piece of Pear wool for vines, letters, pumpkin stem, and leaves
- 1½" × 3" piece of Bittersweet wool for berries
- Hand-sewing supplies (see page 93)
- Freezer paper for transferring patterns
- Glue stick

Cutting

Referring to "Wool Techniques" on page 93, use freezer paper and the patterns on pages 70 and 71 to trace and then cut the appliqués.

From the Old Ivory wool, cut:
1 strip, ⅝" × 9½"; round both ends of the strip
1 pedestal base

From the Parchment wool, cut:
1 pumpkin

From the Pear wool, cut:
1 strip, ⅛" × 12"; taper one end to a point
1 strip, ⅛" × 15"; taper one end to a point
1 stem
8 leaves
GIVE THANKS letters

From the Bittersweet wool, cut:
8 berries

Appliquéing the Wall Hanging

1. Arrange the pedestal base, Old Ivory strip, pumpkin, and stem on the Tobacco wool, referring to the photo on page 68 and the diagram at right. Place the Old Ivory strip for the pedestal top slightly over the pedestal base. Pin in place.

2. Using Summer Brown or coordinating thread and a hand-sewing needle, whipstitch the pedestal base and top, the pumpkin, and the stem in place.

3. Use a running stitch to create the pumpkin ridges; see the photo for stitching placement.

4. Position the Pear strips for vines; add the leaves and berries. Pin and then whipstitch in place.

5. Apply a dab of glue stick on the wrong side of each letter to hold it in place as you stitch. Arrange the letters, extending the *K* and *S* over and below the pedestal. Whipstitch in place.

Color Switch

My preference for dark colors shows up in most of my projects. This one could easily be changed to a brighter colorway, and it may even take on a contemporary look in bold colors.

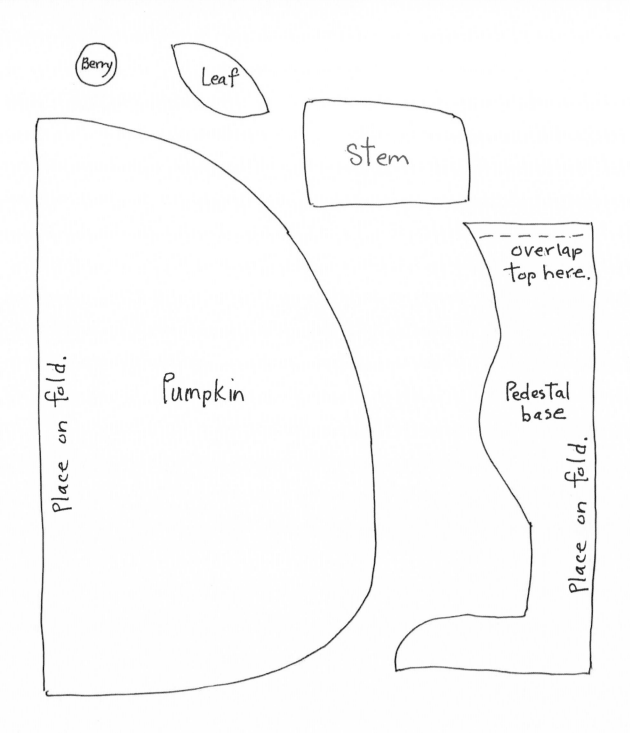

Berry

Leaf

Stem

overlap
top here.

Place on fold.

Pumpkin

Pedestal
base

Place on fold.

Acorn and Oak Leaf

Both acorns and oak leaves are favorites of mine. Acorns, with their variations in size and color, look like tiny sculptures. Oak leaves are sturdy and I love their many shapes.

FINISHED PINCUSHION: 6" high

Materials

I used wool from Blackberry Primitives (see "Resources" on page 95). To help you re-create this project, the materials list gives the exact color names for the wool I used.

- 5" × 8" piece of Parchment wool for acorn
- 2½" × 9" piece of Brown Sugar wool for cap and stem
- 1" × 2" piece of brown homespun cotton for patch
- 5" × 6" piece of Army Green wool for leaves
- 5" × 6" piece of Pear wool for leaves
- Cotton stuffing
- 1 button, ⅜" diameter
- Hand-sewing supplies (see page 93)
- Freezer paper for transferring patterns

Cutting

Referring to "Wool Techniques" on page 93, use freezer paper and the patterns on page 75 to trace and then cut the appliqués.

From the Parchment wool, cut:
2 acorns

From the Brown Sugar wool, cut:
1 strip, 2½" × 8½"
1 strip, ½" × 1½"

From the Army Green wool, cut:
2 oak leaves

From the Pear wool, cut:
2 oak leaves

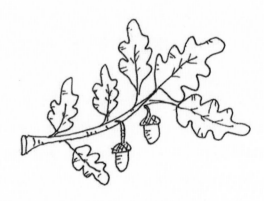

Assembling the Pincushion

1. Layer the acorn pieces and using a scant ¼" seam allowance and Summer Brown or coordinating thread, stitch around the sides and bottom, leaving the top open; knot the thread at each end. Turn right side out and stuff.

2. To create the acorn cap, fold the Brown Sugar wool 2½" × 8½" strip in half crosswise and join the short ends using an ⅛" seam allowance. With the right sides together, slip the cap on the acorn, placing it about ½" below the top edge of the acorn and matching the seamlines. Stitch the cap to the acorn about ¼" from the bottom raw edge, gathering the cap slightly as you stitch. Pull the cap upward over the acorn. Gather the top edge of the acorn cap by stitching a running stitch ¼" from

the top. Pull the gathering thread to draw the top almost closed, turning the raw edge into the center of the cap; do not knot the thread.

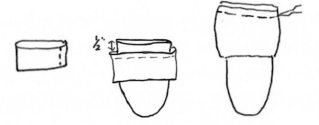

3. Tightly roll the Brown Sugar wool 1" × 1½" strip lengthwise to create a stem. Stitch along the length of the raw edge to prevent it from unrolling. Insert the stem in the acorn cap so 1" is showing, pull tightly on the gathering thread to close the opening, and knot the thread. Stitch around the area again to secure the stem in place.

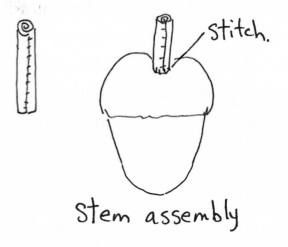

Stem assembly

4. Turn under the raw edges of the homespun patch and press. Place the patch on the lower end of the acorn, crossing over the seam, and whipstitch in place. If desired, create a running stitch X on the patch.

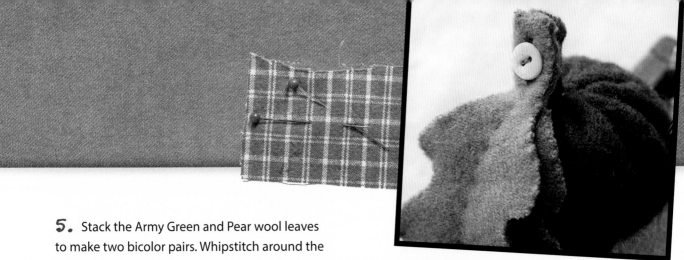

5. Stack the Army Green and Pear wool leaves to make two bicolor pairs. Whipstitch around the edge of each stacked pair to make a finished oak leaf. Use a running stitch to create leaf veins. To join the two finished leaves, whipstitch around the narrow stem areas of both leaves, leaving the curved leaf areas free. To make a buttonhole, center and cut a vertical slit through all four layers, starting about ¼" from the stem end and making the slit about ⅛" larger than the button; be sure to use very sharp scissors. Buttonhole stitch (see page 95) around the raw edges of the buttonhole to stop raveling.

6. Sew the button to the acorn cap stem and then button the leaves onto the stem.

Button Shortcut

As an alternative to a buttonhole on this project, simply attach the oak leaves with a special button, sewing through all oak-leaf layers and the acorn cap stem.

Scant ¼"
seam allowance

Acorn

Oak
leaf

Thankful

In the fall, even a sunny day can turn chilly. The colorful leaves begin to drop, creating great mounds of crunchy leaves on the sidewalks. I actually like walking through these piles—maybe it's a reminder of the childhood joy of running and jumping into the leaves with my sister and brother. Fall also brings the Thanksgiving celebration and a time to be thankful for what we have. This small cornucopia pin keep is a nice reminder of the season.

FINISHED PIN KEEP: 3½" × 5½"

Materials

I used wool from Blackberry Primitives (see "Resources" on page 95). To help you re-create this project, the materials list gives the exact color names for the wool I used.

- 5" × 14" piece of natural coarse linen for cornucopia
- ⅛" × 5" strip of Hazelnut wool for branch
- 1½" × 3" piece of Army Green wool for leaves
- ¾" × 4" strip of Parchment wool for scallop strip
- Cotton stuffing
- Whole cloves (optional)
- Hand-sewing supplies (see page 93)
- Pigma Micron 03 (.35mm) permanent black ink pen
- Freezer paper for transferring patterns

Cutting

Referring to "Wool Techniques" on page 93, use freezer paper and the patterns on page 79 to trace and then cut the cornucopia and wool accents.

From the linen, cut:
2 cornucopias

From the Army Green wool, cut:
3 leaves

From the Parchment wool, cut:
1 scallop strip

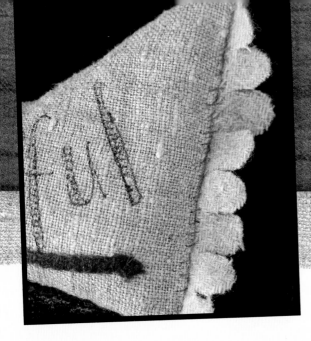

Assembling the Pin Keep

1. Using a window or light box and the black pen, center and trace the *Thankful* letters (page 79) on one cornucopia.

2. Place the cornucopia right sides together. Using a scant ¼" seam allowance, stitch around the curved sides, leaving the straight edge open. At the cornucopia point, take two small stitches across the end to create room for the fabric edges once turned.

3. Turn the cornucopia right side out. Carefully fill the pointed end with stuffing and work your way outward to the opening, adding a few whole cloves if desired. Turn in the raw edge ¼" and whipstitch the opening closed.

Accenting the Pin Keep

1. Position and pin the Hazelnut wool strip below the word *Thankful* to create the branch, referring to the photo on page 76 for placement. Using Summer Brown or coordinating thread and a hand-sewing needle, whipstitch the branch in place.

2. Stitch the three leaves to the end of the branch using a running stitch. Stop the running stitch about halfway up the leaves, leaving the tops free.

3. Pin the scallop strip in place at the straight end of the cornucopia and whipstitch in place.

Crafting with Paper

I am always fascinated with old ledgers, letters, and handwritten documents. Why not use these to create a paper cornucopia? Here's a hint: Any valuable document can be color photocopied, and you can use the copy instead. Cut two cornucopias out of vintage ledger paper, old letters, or journals, omitting the seam allowance. Run a thin line of craft glue just inside the curved edge of one cornucopia, and then gently press the second cornucopia on top, leaving the straight edge open like a pocket. Cut a paper scallop to decorate the opening. Add the name of someone special on the cornucopia and fill it with goodies, sprigs of rosemary, or sweet notes.

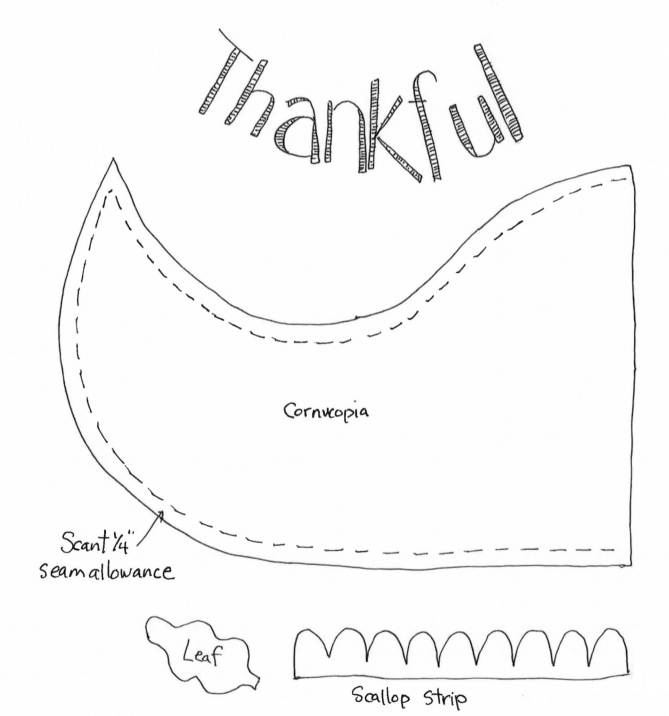

Thankful

Cornucopia

Scant ¼"
seam allowance

Leaf

Scallop Strip

Holly-Days

- -

I like to have a lot of fresh greens and berries around the house for the holidays. Holly is one of my favorite greens, and it is also a favorite to appliqué. The Holly-Days mat can be used as a wall hanging or pillow front or it can be framed.

FINISHED MAT: 14" × 15"

Materials

I used wool from Blackberry Primitives (see "Resources" on page 95). To help you re-create this project, the materials list gives the exact color names for the wool I used.

- 14" × 15" piece of Hickory wool for background
- 3½" × 6" piece of Black wool for urn
- 1" × 9" strip of Brown Sugar wool for stems
- 6" × 12" piece of Pear wool for leaves
- 3" × 5" piece of Red Velvet wool for berries and letters
- Hand-sewing supplies (see page 93)
- Freezer paper for transferring patterns
- Glue stick

Cutting

Referring to "Wool Techniques" on page 93, use freezer paper and the patterns on page 83 to trace and then cut the appliqués.

From the Black wool, cut:
1 urn

From the Brown Sugar wool, cut:
4 strips, ¼" × 9"; crosscut into:
    1 strip, ¼" × 1½"
    2 strips, ¼" × 5"
    1 strip, ¼" × 7"
    1 strip, ¼" × 9"

From the Pear wool, cut:
4 A leaves
2 B leaves
2 C leaves
3 D leaves

From the Red Velvet wool, cut:
4 berries
holly letters

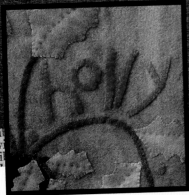

into | w
fr

Appliquéing the Mat

1. Center the urn along the bottom of the Hickory wool, approximately 1" above the edge, and pin in place. Referring to the appliqué placement diagram below, place the Brown Sugar strips at the top edge of the urn, bending them as desired for stems, and pin in place.

2. Using Summer Brown or coordinating thread and a hand-sewing needle, whipstitch the urn and stems in place.

3. Arrange the leaves and berries; pin and then whipstitch in place.

4. Apply a dab of glue stick on the wrong side of each letter to hold it in place as you stitch. Arrange the letters and whipstitch in place.

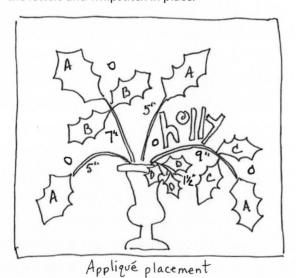

Appliqué placement

5. Use a running stitch to create a vein in the leaves and a single cross-stitch to add dimension to each berry; see the photo on page 80 and "Embroidery Stitches" on page 95.

Holly-Days Extra!

For a fast holiday project, use the Holly-Days design for a stuffed ornament. Cut two pieces of wool, 5" × 7", for the front and back. On the front piece, arrange the letters, two holly leaves, and one berry. Whipstitch the appliqués in place, and then add decorative accent stitching. Layer the front and back, wrong sides together, and whipstitch around the edges, leaving a 2" opening. Add a small amount of stuffing, whipstitch the opening closed, and decorate with a ribbon hanger.

holly

Urn

Berry

Leaf
D

Leaf
C

Leaf
A

Leaf
B

Pinecone and Branch

This little pocket is fun and quick to make—perfect to hang on a peg or doorknob. Add a longer ribbon and show it off as a wearable mini-purse! It's also a great project if you want to tuck in a small gift or candy for a friend. Mine is made from wool with a cotton lining, and I added a buttonhole in case you have a treasure to keep safe inside.

FINISHED POCKET: 4½" × 5¾"

Materials

I used wool from Blackberry Primitives (see "Resources" on page 95). To help you re-create this project, the materials list gives the exact color name for the wool I used.

- 5" × 12" piece of Parchment wool for pocket exterior
- 5" × 12" piece of tan print cotton for lining
- 1" × 4" piece of Hazelnut wool for branch and stem
- 1" × 3" piece of Army Green wool for pine needles
- 3 scraps of different brown wools for pinecone
- 22" length of ⅝"-wide ribbon for hanger
- 1 button, ½" diameter, for closure
- Hand-sewing supplies (see page 93)
- Freezer paper for transferring patterns

Cutting

Referring to "Wool Techniques" on page 93, use freezer paper and the patterns on page 87 to trace and then cut the pinecone appliqués.

From the Hazelnut wool, cut:
1 strip, ¼" × 4"; taper one end
1 strip, ¼" × 1¼"; taper one end

From the Army Green wool, cut:
8 pieces, ¼" × ¾"
5 pieces, ⅛" × ½"

From the brown wool scraps, cut:
1 pinecone base
1 pinecone scallop
1 pinecone top

Appliquéing the Pocket

1. Fold the pocket exterior fabric in half to make a 5" × 6" rectangle. Pin or thread baste along the crease to mark the lower boundary for the pocket front appliqué, then mark a ¼" seam allowance for the top and side boundaries.

2. Arrange the two Hazelnut strips on the exterior so the smaller stem overlaps the branch slightly; refer to the photo on page 84 for placement guidance. Pin in place.

3. Using Summer Brown or coordinating thread and a hand-sewing needle, whipstitch the branch and stem in place.

4. Position the larger Army Green needles along the branch and the smaller needles along the stem. Pin and whipstitch in place.

5. Layer the three brown pinecone pieces; pin and then whipstitch in place.

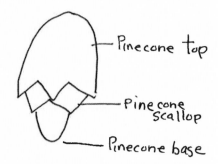

Layered pinecone

Assembling the Pocket

1. Layer the appliquéd pocket exterior with the lining fabric, right sides together. Stitch around three sides using a ¼" seam allowance, leaving one end open for turning.

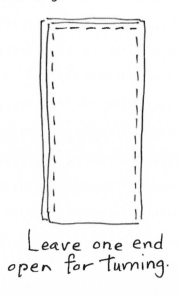

Leave one end open for turning.

2. Turn the pocket right side out and press. Turn in the raw edges along the opening and whipstitch closed.

3. To make the buttonhole, center and cut a vertical slit through both layers of the pocket front, starting about ½" from the top edge of the pocket and making the slit about ⅛" larger than the button; be sure to use very sharp, pointed scissors. Buttonhole stitch (see page 95) around the raw edges of the buttonhole to prevent raveling.

4. Fold the pocket in half so the lining is on the inside. Whipstitch the front and back sides together using small stitches, adding extra stitches at the corners to secure the pocket.

5. Sew the button to the inside of the pocket back, aligning it with the buttonhole on the pocket front (see the photo, above right).

6. To make the ribbon hanger, make a small loop about 2" from each ribbon end, and secure the loop in place with small whipstitches. Referring to the photo above, whipstitch the loops to the side seams of the pocket about ½" below the top edge. Continue stitching the ribbon along the seams, from the loops to the top edge.

Pinecone Top

Pinecone base

Pinecone Scallop

Size Up or Down

This pattern is easy to make either larger or smaller. Just enlarge or reduce the size of the pocket exterior and lining and then adapt the appliqué sizes.

Life Is Good

- -

Today you see chalkboards with handwritten messages everywhere, and this small pillow was designed as a simple place to express your thoughts in wool. I chose Life is good *because I believe it is! Use the thin strips of wool to spell out a customized message. Maybe* Be happy, Love u more, *or* Got wool?

FINISHED PILLOW: 8½" × 10½"

Materials

I used wool from Blackberry Primitives (see "Resources" on page 95). To help you re-create this project, the materials list gives the exact color names for the wool I used.

- 9" × 11" piece of Black wool for pillow front
- 9" × 11" piece of brown homespun for pillow back
- 2" × 14" piece of Parchment wool for letters
- Cotton stuffing
- Hand-sewing supplies (see page 93)
- Fabric glue stick

Cutting

From the Parchment wool, cut:
8 strips, ¼" × 14"

Making the Pillow

1. Referring to the letter placement diagram below, arrange the cut strips to spell out *Life is good* on the Black wool pillow front, trimming and curving the strips as needed to create the letters; apply a dab of glue stick on the wrong side of each letter to hold it in place as you stitch. Narrow strips of wool are very flexible and can be curved easily to make the letters.

2. If using your own sentiment, adapt or sketch out a simple alphabet and plan your word placement, then arrange and glue your letters on the black wool.

letter placement

3. Using Summer Brown or coordinating thread and a hand-sewing needle, whipstitch the letters in place.

4. With right sides together and using a ¼" seam allowance, stitch the pillow front and back together, leaving a 3" opening along the bottom for turning.

5. Turn right side out, stuff, and whipstitch the opening closed.

Be Creative

In creating letters for this project, the only rule I suggest is to keep the strip of wool no wider than ¼". A narrow strip allows more flexibility when you're curving the letters. Make your letters a little wonky, with different sizes and shapes, and don't worry about precision!

Maggie's Favorite Techniques

Here you'll find my favorite wool and hand-sewing supplies, along with techniques to help you create projects that you'll love.

Hand-Sewing Supplies

The supplies I rely on are simple but necessary.

WOOL. My wool choice is 100% wool that's overdyed. I use wool from Blackberry Primitives (see page 94 for the colors used in this book), but you should use colors you love.

THREAD. I use Coats and Clark 100% polyester thread in Summer Brown 54A/8360, and I've used it for 25 years.

COTTON STUFFING. I rely on Sweet Dreams 100% Cotton Stuffing.

NEEDLES. My needles of choice are Sharps size 7.

SCISSORS. You'll need a pair of good-quality sharp snippers. I like 5" scissors for cutting wool pieces. You also may want a pair of scissors for cutting paper. Check out Gingher and Dovo at your local shop; I've used both of those brands with success.

EQUIPMENT. I also use a steam iron, a plastic quilter's ruler (mine is 6" × 24"), pins, and a pincushion. A large magnet is a real help when you spill your pins! I know I'm not the only one who drops pins.

Wool Techniques

When working with patterns (such as shapes and letters), freezer paper is a great way to transfer a design to the wool, and it stabilizes the wool for cutting. Using a window or light box, trace the patterns onto the dull side of the freezer paper. You can cut the pattern pieces right on that line, or you can allow a bit of paper around the design. Press the freezer paper, shiny side down, onto the appropriate wool; wool can be expensive, so don't leave large spaces between each appliqué piece you cut out. Washed and overdyed wool doesn't fray much, so don't worry about the straight of grain when cutting pieces.

One of the many good things about wool appliqué is that you do not need to turn under the raw edges while you appliqué; you just stitch them down. I have used a glue stick to help tack down pieces when I'm stitching so there aren't many pins to tangle with, and I know several people who use a stapler instead. I use a whipstitch for most of my appliqué work, and I accent with a few additional stitches.

When I'm finished with a piece, I may lightly press it with a steam iron to remove any wrinkles. Finishing a wool mat can be as easy as leaving it as is. Sometimes I add a scallop edging, a sawtooth edge, or even lamb's tongues.

For larger pieces, add a cotton backing to stabilize the finished appliqué. With wrong sides together, lay the wool mat on the cotton fabric and cut the fabric at least ½" larger all around. Turn in the raw edge of the cotton fabric and sandwich it between the cotton and the wool so the backing is not visible on the front of the appliqué, then whipstitch it in place. If this is a very large project, I often make a running stitch around the design or the blocks to keep the backing in place.

- -

Wool Color Equivalents

I use wool from Blackberry Primitives because I love their hand-dyed colors. If you'd like to use a different brand, here are the color equivalencies.

Blackberry Primitives Colors	Generic Colors
Army Green	Dark bronzy green
Bittersweet	Rusty orange
Black	Black
Boulder	Beige
Brown Sugar	Dark brown
Chestnut	Rust
Hazelnut	Light brown
Hickory	Medium gray-brown
Ivory	Antique white
Mudslide	Brown-black
Mustard	Mustard
Old Ivory	Tan
Old Straw	Light yellow
Parchment	Light golden tan
Pear	Bronzy green
Red Velvet	Old muted red
Squash	Golden tan
Terra Cotta	Light rust
Tobacco	Dark gray-brown
Waterfall	Soft blue-green

Embroidery Stitches

The following embroidery stitches are used to add details to the projects.

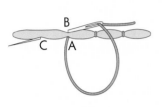

Couching

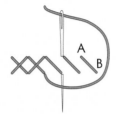

Cross-stitch

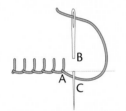

Buttonhole stitch

Running stitch

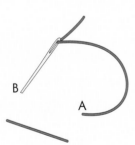

Straight stitch

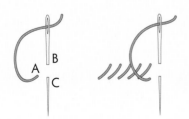

Whipstitch

Resources

Hand-Dyed Wool

Blackberry Primitives

BlackberryPrimitives.com

Marking Pens

Pigma Micron

PigmaMicron.com

Organic Cotton Stuffing

Sweet Dreams 100% Cotton Stuffing

QuiltersDreamBatting.com

Thread

Coats and Clark Dual Duty XP All Purpose 100% Polyester Thread in Summer Brown 54A / 8360

Coats.com

Meet the Author

Maggie Bonanomi

I can't remember a time when I haven't been creating something, whether it was sewing doll clothes with my mother, decorating my room as a teen, or creating things for my home when I got married. My two daughters had their share of handmade items when they were growing up.

I live in the wonderful small town of Lexington, Missouri, in a house built between 1841 and 1845. My hubby and I are celebrating 47 years of marriage as I write this. My daughters are grown with families, and I have grandchildren from the age of two to grown up and married with babies of their own! We got a Westie puppy named Lulu last year, and she continues to bring us joy—and always lets us know who is really in charge!

I'm particularly inspired by the early to mid-nineteenth century, and I like to design what I would want to live with. My colors are dark or muted and the designs are primitive, bordering on traditional. I do not embellish, and I use the same thread, Coats and Clark Summer Brown, because it works so well. When I first began to appliqué, I was more than an hour away from a quilt shop, so I used whatever I had on hand. You can replicate my designs or individualize your projects as you wish, using other stitches or some of the many threads available to embellish your work.

I have a shop called The Purple Turnip, on Main Street in Lexington. It's more of a studio where I get ready for workshops and hold classes, yet it also gives me some shop space for the antiques and old textiles I can barely bear to part with! I enjoy traveling and teaching both appliqué and rug hooking. I get to meet so many people, and the friendships that have developed over the years are very dear to me.

I hope you find time to stitch and make projects that bring you joy. I believe we need to take time to find joy in what we do. I am ever grateful that I have!